STRANGER THINGS

TRIVIA BOOK

A SPECIAL TRIVIA QUIZZES COLLECTION AND FUN FACTS FOR STRANGER THINGS FANS

To the people who are having this book,

We would like to thank you for choosing our product and hope you have a great time with this activity book. Therefore, if you think this book is interesting and you love it, could you please give a minute to share your thinking on Amazon. That would be so grateful to us and we appreciate your support a lot.

Thanks so much and wish you all the best.

TABLE OF CONTENT

This Brilliant Trivia Book belongs to

....

CHAPTER 1

WELCOME

LET'S QUIZZ!

1. What kind of film is Stranger Things?

   A. Science fiction and horror

   B. Horror and cartoon

   C. Cartoon and sitcom

   D. Sitcom

2. What is the original country of Stranger Things?

   A. England

   B. America

   C. Singapore

   D. Russian

3. Who is the creator of Stranger Things?

    A. The Duffer Brothers

    B. Winona Ryder

    C. David Harbour

    D. Finn Wolfhard

4. The Office originally aired on NBC.

    A. True

    B. False

5. How many seasons does Stranger Things have?

    A. 1

    B. 3

    C. 7

    D. 9

6. How many episodes does Stranger Things have?

    A. 18

    B. 19

    C. 20

    D. 25

7. English is the original language of Stranger Things.

    A. True

    B. False

8. How many episodes in season 1?

    A. 2

    B. 4

    C. 6

    D. 8

9. How many episodes in season 2?

    A. 7

    B. 8

    C. 9

    D. 10

10. How many episodes in season 3?

    A. 1

    B. 4

    C. 6

    D. 8

11. When did season 1 release?

    A. July 15th, 2016

    B. August 15th, 2016

    C. September 15th, 2016

    D. October 15th, 2016

12. When did season 2 release?

    A. August 27th, 2017

    B. September 27th, 2017

    C. October 27th, 2017

    D. November 27th, 2017

13. When did season 3 release?

    A. May 4th, 2019

    B. June 4th, 2019

    C. July 4th, 2019

    D. August 4th, 2019

14. Stranger Things is set in the fictional rural town of Hawkins, Indiana, during the early 1980s.

    A. True

    B. False

15. When is Will's birthday?

   A. January 22nd

   B. February 22nd

   C. March 22nd

   D. April 22nd

16. How old is Will in season 1?

   A. 12

   B. 13

   C. 14

   D. 15

17. How old is Will in season 2?

   A. 12

   B. 13

   C. 14

   D. 15

18. How old is Will in season 3?

   A. 12

   B. 13

   C. 14

   D. 15

19. Who is Will's father?

    A. Lonnie

    B. Jonathan

    C. Max

    D. Troy

20. Who is Will's brother?

    A. Lonnie

    B. Jonathan

    C. Max

    D. Troy

21. Who is Will's mother?

    A. Darlence

    B. Eleven

    C. Joyce

    D. James

22. Who is Will's housemate?

    A. Darlence

    B. Eleven

    C. Joyce

    D. James

23. Eleven is also Will's friend.

   A. True

   B. False

24. Who is Will's great aunt?

   A. Darlence

   B. Eleven

   C. Joyce

   D. James

25. Who is Will's best friend?

   A. Mike Wheeler

   B. Dustin Henderson

   C. Lucas Sinclair

   D. All of the above

CHAPTER 1

WELCOME

ANSWERS ARE COMING!!

1. A. Science fiction and horror

2. B. America

3. A. The Duffer Brothers

4. B. False

5. B. 3

6. D. 25

7. A. True

8. D. 8

9. C. 9

10. D. 8

11. A. July 15th, 2016

12. C. October 27th, 2017

13. C. July 4th, 2019

14. A. True

15. C. March 22nd

16. A. 12

17. B. 13

18. C. 14

19. A. Lonnie

20. B. Jonathan

21. C. Joyce

22. B. Eleven

23. A. True

24. A. Darlence

25. D. All of the above

DID YOU KNOW?

➢ The show is based on a real time travel project.

➢ Stranger Things is based on real conspiracy theories about the United States government conducting reality-bending experiments on children.

➢ The show was also initially called Montauk and set on the far edge of the Long Island peninsula

CHAPTER 2

HI WILL!
LET'S QUIZZ!

1. What color is Will's eyes?

   A. Red

   B. Brown

   C. Blue

   D. Green

2. What color is Will's hair?

   A. Red

   B. Brown

   C. Blue

   D. Green

3. How tall is Will?

    A. 5'1"

    B. 5'2"

    C. 5'3"

    D. 5'4"

4. How heavy is Will?

    A. 73.1 lbs

    B. 74.1 lbs

    C. 75.1 lbs

    D. 76.1 lbs

5. What is Will's characteristic?

    A. Soft-spoken

    B. Amicable

    C. Honest

    D. All of the above

6. What is Will's favorite?

    A. Science

    B. Math

    C. History

    D. Music

7. Will is a member of their school's AV club.

    A. True

    B. False

8. When is Mike's birthday?

    A. January 7th

    B. March 7th

    C. April 7th

    D. May 7th

9. How old is Mike in season 1?

    A. 12

    B. 13

    C. 14

    D. 15

10. How old is Mike in season 2?

    A. 12

    B. 13

    C. 14

    D. 15

11. Will's father always treats him with full loving.

    A. True

    B. False

12. How old is Mike in season 3?

    A. 11

    B. 12

    C. 13

    D. 14

13. Who is the person that Mike has a crush on?

    A. Nancy

    B. Eleven

    C. Max

    D. Kali

14. Who is Mike's dad?

    A. Rin

    B. Ted

    C. Lucas

    D. Gerald

15. Who is Mike's mom?

    A. Nancy

    B. Jenny

    C. Besty

    D. Karen

16. How many sisters does Mike have?

    A. 1

    B. 2

    C. 3

    D. 4

17. Holly is one of Mike's sisters.

    A. True

    B. False

18. Who is Mike's sister?

    A. Nancy

    B. Jenny

    C. Besty

    D. Karen

19. Who is Mike's best friend?

    A. Will

    B. Lucas

    C. Dustin

    D. All of the above

20. Mike is a student at Hawkins Middle School

    A. True

    B. False

21. What color is Mike's hair?

    A. Dark blonde

    B. Dark red

    C. Dark brown

    D. Dark blue

22. What color is Mike's eyes?

    A. Black

    B. Brown

    C. Green

    D. Blue

23. How tall is Mike?

    A. 5'5"

    B. 5'6"

    C. 5'7"

    D. 5'8"

24. In the first season. Eleven wore a pink dress, who is the owner of that dress?

    A. Pam

    B. Karen

    C. Katy

    D. Nancy

25. Mike is shown to be optimistic, morally compassionate, and highly committed to his friends

    A. True

    B. False

CHAPTER 2

HI WILL!

ANSWERS ARE COMING!!

1.   B. Brown

2.   B. Brown

3.   D. 5'4"

4.   A. 73.1 lbs

5.   D. All of the above

6.   A. Science

7.   A. True

8.   C. April 7th

9.   A. 12

10. B. 13

11. B. False

12. D. 14

13. B. Eleven

14. B. Ted

15. D. Karen

16. B. 2

17. A. True

18. D. Karen

19. D. All of the above

20. A. True

21. C. Dark brown

22. B. Brown

23. D. 5'8"

24. D. Nancy

25. A. True

DID YOU KNOW?

➤ They auditioned 906 boys and 307 girls for the main roles.

➤ The Duffer brothers and casting director Carmen Cuba undertook the gargantuan task of hearing from 1213 child actors to get the right people for what would be crucial roles

CHAPTER 3

BROTHERHOOD
LET'S QUIZZ!

1. Who was often dismissive of her brother, calling him "gross" and a "douchebag",

    A. Nancy

    B. Eleven

    C. Erica

    D. Kali

2. What is the other name of Eleven?

    A. Jane

    B. Hana

    C. Jenny

    D. Stella

3. Who is the voice actor of Eleven?

    A. Millie Bobby Brown

    B. Natalie Portman

    C. Jennifer Lawrence

    D. Viola Davis

4. What is Eleven's characteristic?

    A. Timid

    B. Protective

    C. Caution

    D. All of the above

5. Who is the person that Eleven fell in love with?

    A. Will

    B. Mike

    C. Max

    D. Lucas

6. Eleven was taught how to read and signal Morse code by Hopper

    A. True

    B. False

7. While living in the woods for a month, Eleven learned crucial survival skills, such as hunting (by using her powers) and how to make a fire.

    A. True

    B. False

8. What is the date when Will Byers goes missing?

    A. September 6th, 1983

    B. October 6th, 1983

    C. November 6th, 1983

    D. December 6th, 1983

9. Who is the person that races with Will in episode 1?

    A. Lucas

    B. Mike

    C. Hopper

    D. Dustin

10. What does Will want if he win this race?

    A. A comic

    B. A bike

    C. A teddy bear

    D. A wand

11. X-Men 134 is the name of a comic.

    A. True

    B. False

12. Whose comic is?

    A. Roy

    B. Lucas

    C. Dustin

    D. Will

13. What is the name of the road that Will usually go home from Mike's?

    A. Mirkwood

    B. High Street

    C. Catwood

    D. Big Road Street

14. When Jonathan listen this song, he remember Will. What song is it?

    A. Should I stay or should I go

    B. Thank you for being a friend

    C. You can't always get what you want

    D. Beautiful

15. Erica is Lucas's sister.

    A. True

    B. False

16. Where does Barb her thumb?

    A. At Max's house

    B. At Lucas's house

    C. At Will's house

    D. At Steve's house

17. How does Barb cut her thumb?

    A. Cutting open a beer can

    B. Picking up a broken glass bottle

    C. Using knife

    D. She doesn't know

18. Who can crush a soda can with her mind?

    A. Erica

    B. Robin

    C. Eleven

    D. Karen

19. Where does she crush that soda?

A. In a park

B. In a room

C. In a playground

D. In hospital

20. What is the brand of that soda?

A. 7 up

B. Twice

C. Coca-Cola

D. Water

21. How many messages does Will spell out when using Joyce's Christmas lights?

A. 1

B. 2

C. 3

D. 4

22. " Right here" and "Run" are those messages.

A. True

B. False

23. When goes to the school with Mike and friends, what name does Eleven use?

A. Elena

B. Eleanor

C. Elevator

D. Elip

24. What does Hopper find when he opens Will's body

A. Bottle

B. Can

C. Cotton stuffing

D. Knife

25. Filling the sentence: Dustin can't wait to tell Will that _____ was crying at his funeral.

A. Jane Ives

B. Jennifer Hayes

C. Lucas Sinclair

D. Mike Wheeler

CHAPTER 3

BROTHERHOOD

ANSWERS ARE COMING!!

1.   A. Nancy

2.   A. Jane

3.   A. Millie Bobby Brown

4.   D. All of the above

5.   B. Mike

6.   A. True

7.   A. True

8.   C. November 6th,1983

9.   D. Dustin

10.   A. A comic

11.   A. True

12.   C. Dustin

13.   A. Mirkwood

14.   A. Should I stay or should I go

15.   A. True

16.   D. At Steve's house

17.   A. Cutting open a beer can

18.   C. Eleven

19.   B. In a room

20.   C. Coca-Cola

21.   B. 2

22.   A. True

23.   B. Eleanor

24.   C. Cotton stuffing

25.   B. Jennifer Hayes

DID YOU KNOW?

➢ The show was almost an anthology series with different characters and settings every season

➢ The show would have said goodbye to Eleven, Dustin, Will, Mike, Lucas, and the rest of the cast after the first season.

CHAPTER 4

WHY DID YOU COME HERE?
LET'S QUIZZ!

1. Who placed a bug in Hopper's house?

    A. Will

    B. Eleven

    C. Hawkins

    D. Mike

2. Where is that bug?

    A. TV

    B. Washing machine

    C. Cupboard

    D. Ceiling light

3. Eleven steals 4 boxes of Eggos from a store.

    A. True

    B. False

4. Why do Steve and his friends spray paint the movie theater sign?

    A. To embarrass Eleven

    B. To embarrass Mike

    C. To embarrass Erika

    D. To embarrass Nancy

5. What is that movie name, which is displaying?

    A. Harry Porter

    B. All the right moves

    C. The golden ring

    D. Stranger things

6. What words do Steve and his friends spray?

    A. Starring Eleven the slut wheeler

    B. Starring Mike the slut wheeler

    C. Starring Erika the slut wheeler

    D. Starring Nancy the slut wheeler

7. Lucas is very good at using his Wrist-Rocket slingshot

   A. True

   B. False

8. What does Lucas use the Wrist-Rocket for?

   A. Fight enemies

   B. Protect his friends

   C. Buying food

   D. A&B

9. While floating in the homemade sensory deprivation tank, where does Eleven find Will in the Upside Down?

   A. In his house

   B. In his garden

   C. Inside Castle Byers

   D. In a cave

10. What items does Dustin and Lucas steal from school's canteen?

   A. Chocolate pudding

   B. Candy

   C. Ice cream

   D. Water bottle

11. If Eleven hangs on a little longer after fighting Dr. Brenner, what Mike will do for her?

    A. They can go to the Ice Castle

    B. They can go to the Snow Ball

    C. They can go to the Secret Forest

    D. They can go to the Town Hall

12. What does Nancy give Jonathan as a Christmas gift?

    A. A new car

    B. A new bike

    C. A new camera

    D. A new mobile phone

13. What is Brad's full name?

    A. Brad Smith

    B. Brad Ryder

    C. Brad Sinclair

    D. Brad Holland

14. What film that Joyce buy tickets is

    A. The golden ring

    B. Poltergeist

    C. How I meet your mother

    D. The last laugh

15. Where was Max originally from?

   A. Boston

   B. New York

   C. Ohio

   D. California

16. In October of 1984, Max began attending Hawkins Middle School.

   A. True

   B. False

17. Where does Max kiss Lucas?

   A. Snow Ball

   B. Town Hall

   C. Grocery Store

   D. Pharmacy

18. Who is Max's biology mom?

   A. Billy

   B. Alice

   C. Susan

   D. Annie

19. Who is Max's biology dad?

   A. Sam

   B. Harry

   C. Henry

   D. Rin

20. Who is Max's best friends?

   A. Nate

   B. Will

   C. Lucas

   D. All of the above

21. What color is Max's hair?

   A. Pink

   B. Red

   C. Blue

   D. Blonde

22. Max has got blue's eyes color.

   A. True

   B. False

23. What sport does Max like?

    A. Racing

    B. Skateboarding

    C. Skipping

    D. Dancing

24. Max is a tomboy

    A. True

    B. False

25. What does Max need to unlock the door of the AV club?

    A. Her mind

    B. A fake key

    C. Water bottle

    D. Paper clip

CHAPTER 4

WHY DID YOU COME HERE?

ANSWERS ARE COMING!!

1. C. Hawkins

2. D. Ceiling light

3. A. True

4. D. To embarrass Nancy

5. D. All the right moves

6. D. Starring Nancy the slut wheeler

7. A. True

8. D. A&B

9. C. Inside Castle Byers

10. A. Chocolate pudding

11. B. They can go to the Snow Ball

12. C. A new camera

13. B. Brad Holland

14. B. Poltergeist

15. D. California

16. A. True

17. A. Snow Ball

18. C. Susan

19. A. Sam

20. D. All of the above

21. B. Red

22. A. True

23. B. Skateboarding

24. A. True

25. D. Paper clip

DID YOU KNOW?

➢ Dacre Montgomery played the greasy-headed Billy Hargrove in the second season.

➢ The character was a nod to the classic Stephen King villain Randall Flagg, who has appeared in several of the author's novels. But in his audition, Montgomery channeled a lot of other demons. He read through the prepared scenes

CHAPTER 5

DON'T MOVE
LET'S QUIZZ!

1. All the kids in Stranger Things are friends in real life.

   A. True

   B. False

2. Eleven doesn't have this name.

   A. El

   B. Eleanor

   C. Davey

   D. The Weirdo

3. What is Eleven's power?

    A. Flying

    B. Super speed

    C. Using her mind to control things

    D. Looking at a long distance

4. What is the name of other dimension in Stranger Things?

    A. The Stranger zone

    B. The Outside

    C. The Inside

    D. The Upside Down

5. What game is Mike good at?

    A. Chess

    B. Dungeons and Dragons

    C. Rock paper scissors

    D. Tic tac toe

6. Eggos is a delicious waffle.

    A. True

    B. False

7. Where is the opening scene taking place?

    A. Will's bed room

    B. Lab

    C. School

    D. Park

8. What is Eleven's favorite food?

    A. Egoos

    B. Chicken

    C. Ice cream

    D. Curry

9. What is the name of faceless creature?

    A. Forgiveness

    B. Dragon

    C. Demogorgon

    D. Faceless

10. Mirkwood is used as an escape road for Eleven and friends

    A. True

    B. False

11. Joyce communicate with Will by using Christmas Lights.

    A. True

    B. False

12. What animal is Yurtle?

    A. Turtle

    B. Kitten

    C. Dog

    D. Bat

13. What animal is Tews?

    A. Turtle

    B. Kitten

    C. Dog

    D. Bat

14. Who is the person that Dustin has a crush in?

    A. Nancy

    B. Stella

    C. Alice

    D. Suzie

15. Lucas is a student at Hawkins Middle School

    A. True

    B. False

16. What color is Lucas's eyes?

    A. Black

    B. Brown

    C. Green

    D. Blue

17. Where is the gate to the Upside Down?

    A. At Will's bed room

    B. At school gate

    C. Behind the big tree in the backyard of school

    D. At Hawkins Lab

18. What color is Lucas's hair?

    A. Black

    B. Brown

    C. Green

    D. Blue

19. At which grade did Lucas meet Mike and Will?

    A. 1st

    B. 2nd

    C. 3rd

    D. 4th

20. What do the boys call the Mind Flayer?

    A. Shadow Monster

    B. Light Monster

    C. Blue Monster

    D. Fat Monster

21. In season 2, what is the name of the game that the boys play at the arcade?

    A. Plants vs. Zombie

    B. Dig Dug

    C. Dungeons & Dragons

    D. Badminton

22. How old is Johnathan in season 1?

    A. 15

    B. 16

    C. 17

    D. 18

23. How old is Johnathan in season 2?

    A. 15

    B. 16

    C. 17

    D. 18

24. Who is Johnathan's girlfriend?

    A. Nancy

    B. Bella

    C. Stella

    D. Annie

25. What does Bob wear at Halloween Party?

    A. Spider Man

    B. Iron Man

    C. Ant Man

    D. Count Dracula

CHAPTER 5

DON'T MOVE

ANSWERS ARE COMING!!

1. A. True

2. C. Davey

3. C. Using her mind to control things

4. D. The Upside Down

5. B. Dungeons and Dragons

6. A. True

7. B. Lab

8. A. Egoos

9. C. Demogorgon

10. A. True

11. A. True

12. A. Turtle

13. B. Kitten

14. D. Suzie

15. A. True

16. D. .Blue

17. D. At Hawkins Lab

18. B. Brown

19. D. 4th

20. A. Shadow Monster

21. B. Dig Dug

22. B.1 6

23. C. 17

24. A. Nancy

25. D. Count Dracula

DID YOU KNOW?

➤ In the first season, Eleven dons a pink dress and absurd blonde wig in an homage to E.T., but the Easter egg is also a clue to her entire, otherworldly character.

➤ Brown once showed up to set covered in glitter.

CHAPTER 6

SEE YOU LATER
LET'S QUIZZ!

1. 'Stranger Things' was originally going to be called 'Montauk.'

    A. True

    B. False

2. What color is Johnathan's eyes?

    A. Black

    B. Brown

    C. Blue

    D. Green

3. What color is Johnathan's hair?

   A. Red

   B. Blue

   C. Brown

   D. Black

4. How many poster in Johnathan's bedroom?

   A. 2

   B. 4

   C. 6

   D. 8

5. Johnathan's family has a dog.

   A. True

   B. False

6. In season 2, where do Steve and Nancy break up?

   A. At a park

   B. At supermarket

   C. In a bathroom

   D. At company

7. Nancy is a skilled detective.

   A. True

   B. False

8. How do the boys communicate with others

   A. Email

   B. Via Walkie - talkie

   C. Skype

   D. Their mind

9. What song does Toto play when Nabcy and Steve are studying in her room?

   A. European

   B. Asia

   C. Africa

   D. America

10. What is Alexie's nationality?

   A. English

   B. American

   C. Singaporean

   D. Russian

11. Nancy is good at short gun and handgun.

    A. True

    B. False

12. Who is Nancy's best friend?

    A. Tommy

    B. Tom

    C. Bruce

    D. Barbara

13. Who together with Joyce kidnap Alexei?

    A. Jim

    B. Will

    C. Max

    D. Michael

14. What does Alexei do?

    A. Businessman

    B. Pilot

    C. Scientist

    D. Singer

15. Jim Hopper's nickname in "Stranger Things" is Hop.

    A. True

    B. False

16. Where is the Key machine?

    A. Under a tree

    B. In a tree house

    C. In classroom

    D. Under the mall

17. Where does Eleven steals fries?

    A. Stella's Burgers

    B. Benny's Burgers

    C. Jim's Burgers

    D. Alice's Burgers

18. Where does the boys discover Eleven?

    A. In the woods

    B. In the school

    C. In a park

    D. Near a river

19. The Palace is the name of the arcade.

    A. True

    B. False

20. What song does Dustin sing at the end of season 3?

    A. The sun

    B. Happy ending

    C. The never-ending story

    D. Welcome home

21. How many languages does Robin speak?

    A. 1

    B. 2

    C. 3

    D. 4

22. Where does Billy work?

    A. Hawkins Community Football Yard

    B. Hawkins Community Pool

    C. Hawkins Community Hall

    D. Hawkins Community Canteen

23. What does Jim Hopper do?

    A. Police

    B. Pilot

    C. Chef

    D. Teacher

24. Where do Nancy and Jonathan work?

    A. The Hawkins Hospital

    B. The Hawkins Post

    C. The Hawkins Restaurant

    D. The Hawkins Hall

25. 1980 Chevy Blazer is the truck that Jim drives

    A. True

    B. False

CHAPTER 6

SEE YOU LATER

ANSWERS ARE COMING!!

1. A. True

2. B. Brown

3. C. Brown

4. A .2

5. A. True

6. C. In a bathroom

7. A. True

8. B. Via Walkie - talkie

9. C. Africa

10. D. Russian

11. A. True

12. D. Barbara

13. A. Jim

14. C. Scientist

15. A. True

16. D. Under the mall

17. B. Benny's Burgers

18. A. In the woods

19. A. True

20. The never-ending story

21. D.4

22. C. Hawkins Community Pool

23. D. Police

24. B. The Hawkins Post

25. A. True

DID YOU KNOW?

➢ The gang went trick-or-treating together.

➢ It's probably a lot easier to remain anonymous when you're behind a mask, even if you're on a wildly popular Netflix show. All the kids are famous for being friends in real life, and they've even adventured out on Halloween together

Made in the USA
Coppell, TX
13 November 2022

86288415R00056